Walking By the Waves

Shikha

BlueRose Publishers

First Published in January 2021

ISBN: 978-93-5427-073-4

BLUEROSE PUBLISHERS

www.bluerosepublishers.com

info@bluerosepublishers.com

+91 8882 898 898

Cover Design:

Shivangi Lohia

Typographic Design:

Deepika Matpal

Distributed by: BlueRose, Amazon, Flipkart, Shopclues

To my creators,

Parul & Yogesh.

To my constant,

My brother,

Krunal.

And my forever,

Maunik.

The biggest truth in life is -

everyone's truth is different,

yet, it is true!

Preface

The idea of this book is almost a decade old, though it started taking shape only a year ago. I clearly remember it was a Sunday morning, when on impulse I decided to write a book of poems. I went over my old journals and some notes, and astonishingly, I rumbled upon a couple of verses, which I could still connect to. Several of these were written as late as 2019-2020. The purpose of this book is to connect to individual's fervor thereby experiencing unique emotions at different phases of their life. I assure, each one of you will be able to connect to at least a few verses. Although the verses are quotidian, they are satisfying when read loud. The book is designed in 6 sections, each section with its own proem. Each section, discloses the truths of many, yet signalizes that, "the many" fail to understand when their fellows go through the same. This book is about being sensitive to ourselves as well as others. Treating right our fellow being is never the unnerving topic until you get mistreated. Whether you feel broken, or in love, or happy, or you question the stereotypical beliefs, this book will assure you that its ok to feel all of that. Every escapade defining your act/ mood on daily basis is unique. No story can entirely be the same, yet the agonies and ecstasies can befriend each other. And that's the aim of this book, to be your constant companion in this journey called "phase of life". No matter how old you are or how seasoned you are or what gender/ culture/ ethnicity you belong to, yet it hurts the same and our spirits feel elated the same way. The commonness of suffering and gaiety, is uncommon.

Its brave to confront your past and accept your fears of the daunting future; and yet be lucid.

Happy reading,

Shikha

Acknowledgements

"It has been said that we need just three things in life: Something to do, something to look forward to and someone to love".

- Maya Angelou

Foremost, I am indebted to Reshmi and Siddhesh without whose heartening motivation, I wouldn't have ever thought of getting published. Reshmi, I have learnt a lot from you since we first started working together. Siddhesh, you have been a friend and support since my first poem.

A huge thanks to Abhilash Gangadhar for allowing me, so lovingly, to use his photographs.

I would like to thank (and hug) Nour Jabbour for taking out the time to read my final manuscript and giving an honest opinion. You were the last drop of confidence I needed.

And finally, a shout to my super cool parents, brother and partner who never miss a chance to show their totally biased love for me. You are my rock.

The alluring expanse of my heart

Why obliterate your mind of those beautiful expressions and emotions, just to "be in the moment". My mind is my palace and my heart its queen; I can't tame my queen to feel what spectators say is "right". Once you decide to break the chains and just be, your imagination and intelligence will see no bounds. Your mind does not follow any quick-fix recipes to not feel, when it hurts. Here, I am presenting an anthology of my poems (I hope I can write more too), with the hope to connect to all, through my words and verses.

Although the genres of poems are varied; my verses try to deliver a string message to its readers - Its ok to live in the dream for a while. Its ok to feel what you feel. Its ok to not be able to process situations as soon as they happen. And finally, its ok to be deceived and be hurt than to have never been loved. Love is the simplest complicated human idea. One will have opinions and philosophies on love, but none can deny its existence. Such is my ideation of love and deception, having grown up reading Rumi. Rumi has been a constant inspiration since my first poem.

"If you're not in love, you have missed your goal.

He calls! The breeze of love must find your soul.

Glory resurrected you, glory made you whole!

If you're not in love, life passes you by".

- Rumi

Table of Contents

Book I

You are Wine.

Love & More.

A moth has a life of a few days, so the moth makes sure not to spend a minute of it in darkness. The moth has seen several of its fellows dying in the light, yet with no fear, the moth pursues light. The moth is my teacher.

The following love poems are model of our heart's imbecile emotions. It keeps changing. You feel so elated by a person today (when you are 25), but might feel indifferent at 60. The emotions of a person truly alive, keeps changing. It's a sign. It's a gift.

Experience love and more!

What a morning would that be

I am greedy.

After your call - in the morning,

I started day-dreaming –

About when we would wake up next to each other – naked,

and complete.

That day,

The sun would shine brighter,

The winds would be gentler,

The stars won't yet be ready - to yet say "Goodbye".

What a morning would that be!

First Love

I loved it when he said -

I came in his dream.

I loved it more,

When he said -

I am his dream.

Shameless

My girlfriends warned me.

Everyone warned me - of love.

It takes away everything,

Your spirit,

Your faith,

It will be the path to your grave, they said,

I heard all -

Listened none.

I shamelessly gave myself,

Wanting to die in his arms.

You will always be mine

There he was,

In the street, brimming among faces.

Yet I could spot him audibly.

Could feel the curves of his smile.

The cravings of his eyes -

From skies afar.

I am here, with someone and you have your someone.

I love my someone but,

A part of that love -

Is you.

You will always be mine – first.

New love(s)

Love is different for all.

It always will be.

The images of,

Romeo and Juliet,

Laila and Majnu,

Then the ideas of Rumi and Hafez,

The wisdom of Dickinson -

But when it will come to you,

It will still be blue,

And new.

Never stop loving yourself

Over the time,

Out of all the people,

I have known

I miss me the most.

My face

Each memory of yours,

Is a wrinkle less on my face.

Institution of marriage

Yes, I am committed.

Not to him,

Not in a relationship,

Not at all to his family,

But only to our happiness and peace.

If he is happier away from me,

My fidelity lets him go.

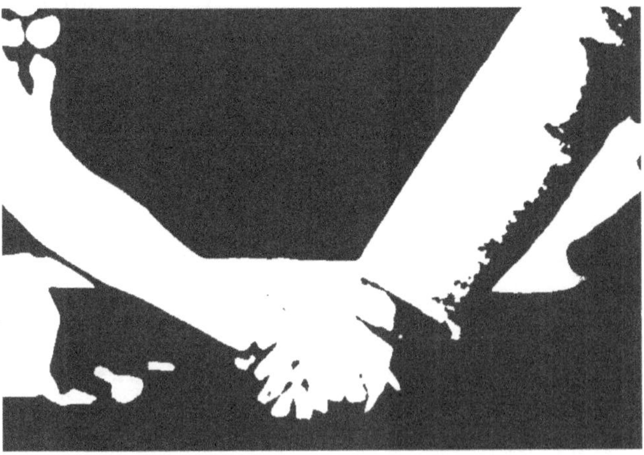

Love in the first hour

It was exactly 70,738 hours back,

When we first fell in love,

Somehow, it still feels like that first hour.

18th October

We found each other in the busiest crowd.

Our eyes met,

We glanced,

My heart felt alive again.

I understood the people singing and dancing deranged,

In those movies.

I understood music,

And I was never the same again.

He is my study

Don't think I gave myself to him to be loved back.

There is much more

He makes me calm,

He makes me bold,

And the pride molds.

He manifests – content.

He is my study.

Toxicity

I forgot I liked winters more, while gazing at the sun - bare.

I forgot that mangoes were my favorite, while feeding you the sweetest rare.

I forgot that I hated beaches, while walking in the sandy breezes.

I forgot that I too had dust allergies, while keeping you away from wheezes.

I forgot that I too was afraid of heights, while holding you up the freezes.

I forgot myself, while making your life easy.

That first

I am not sure -

What it meant!

Was it to bind me forever,

Or set me free.

I am not sure –

How it feels!

Was he always in me,

Or never existed.

Our indelible kiss

Each nerve in my body unnerves.

The blood flushes to every living muscle,

It is not the feeling of nearness,

But the feeling I recall when your lips touched mine.

You are important

I feel happy when I see you,

I feel happy when you are not around - in the hope that you will appear anytime.

I feel happy when my fingers touch your handsome face,

I feel complete with you.

I don't know -

How,

When,

You became my "only"!

Content

Hold me like this,

To lift a crystal like,

No rush, eyes bright,

So fulfilled.

Tough

Let my life leave too when you leave me;

But if you leave me half way, I will fight the world to get you back;

I will bring you back from up the paradise;

But not let your life egress without mine.

Great together

When I think about you,

I have no regrets,

No anger now,

No complaints,

No hurt,

Just a knowing smile,

Recalling, we were really great together!

Deceit & More Ache.

There is familiarity in that one person whom you desire to share your secrets with, until they deceive you, leave you, make you just a shoddy calculation in their expensive lives. For me, deceit is a natural human experience, similar to love. The feeling of deception surely dwindles if we treat all fellow aliens with a friendly sense of warmth.

The poems in this section are a model of the screams of our minds. Suffering is a connection to your soul; makes you see your real self. Let it flow, let us embrace it.

"So we choose a tiny seed to be devoted to.

This body, one path or one teacher.

Look wider and farther".

- Rumi

Borrowed love

He had magic touch.

Though short yet the most amazing date.

We ate,

Made love,

He owned me – in that moment.

We felt complete.

The next morning was as beautiful,

We went back home to our "lovers".

They all leave, after all

He loved me -

I can tell.

He praised me - told all his friends.

He said he has never seen a girl like me,

He was satisfied – love making,

He loved the food I cooked,

Yet he went home the next day.

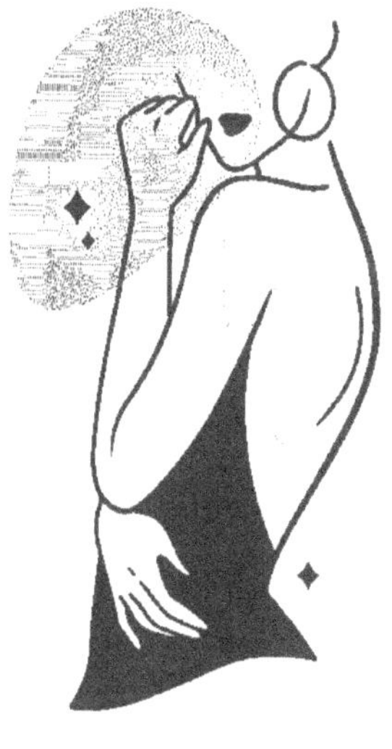

This morning

That morning -

When we made love,

The sun shone brighter,

I felt numb with passion.

This morning -

When we are no more,

The sun still shines bright,

I feel numb with sorrow.

Your lies

Do you remember!

You told me,

You loved me -

Like no one before.

And will do till the last breath,

And that I am the "only one".

Well!

I believed you.

A Shout

I can’t love you.

I pity you!

Yes, I pity you!

Because you didn’t believe in me – when you did - it was too late,

Because you didn’t value me,

Because you didn’t choose me,

Because you couldn’t see what strangers could easily see in my eyes,

Yes, I pity you!

Because you didn’t take me seriously,

Because you never observed the wet pillows in the morning – right next to you,

Because you claimed to love me – yet hurt me,

Because you believed in their lies and not me,

Yes, I pity you!

Because you believed you didn’t have any option – though you always had,

Because one day you will realize what you lost – and I won't be around to cry with you,

Because you had the power to make me the happiest person – yet you chose not to,

Because in you I had my trust – which you broke,

I can't love you,

I have nothing left,

All I can give you is – my PITY!

The moment

The moment you looked into my eyes,

And couldn't see me crying,

I knew you lost me.

I know you, I know your type

I will not admit to love you -

Never.

Because if I do,

You will crush me,

And break me.

“Us”

I can literally feel the rush of blood in my eyes,

For each time you didn’t choose “us”.

Not Whole

I needed you then,

But you believed not in me – but them.

I loved you then,

But you chose to be blind.

They are fooling you – I warned,

Yet, you chose their lies over my truth.

Times have changed.

You now know – the truth,

You are hurt – you need me now.

I am still here, but not whole.

Know it

Stars are not infinite,

And so, is not the sky.

Honey is not the sweetest,

And so, is not sugar.

Money does not give happiness,

And so, doesn't love.

A broken heart yields poetry,

And so, does a happy mind.

Futile relationships give you pain,

And so, does blood relatives.

Don't lie to yourself,

Lies bring grief.

Futile relationships

At times, a friend who knows you,

Will bring you pain,

Grief,

Disappointments,

Than a stranger who would see through you – in the moment.

Relationships are two-way street

The problem is not the little sacrifices she attempts to, every day. She loves it. She measures her life through those moments. She loves every bit of it. But when he shuts her out completely every now and then; she fears losing herself in the relationship.

Balance

I am scared to argue with you,

Not to argue is yet dangerous,

How to dissolve – someone please tell!

The fine balance between maintaining peace and giving up hope!

Without you

While you were busy mending others,

I learnt to make a family without you.

While you were busy not hearing my screams,

I learnt to be happy without you.

While you were busy taking me for granted,

I learnt to live without you.

Tired

It bleeds away all my vigor to not feel, what I feel!

Agony & Freedom

In the palace of pain, the wind which blows the windows shut, also opens it. Such is a miracle of defeating grief. The sphere you see, reading these poems, falls in the region of both of our minds.

The poems in this section are a model of the immense store of experiences, where we are all wounded. Let's celebrate the freedom of those who got through and the journey of those who are still to get over.

Let's open the mouth-cage and fly away!

"The idea is to write it so that people hear it and it slides through the brain and goes straight to the heart".

- Maya Angelou

Lost to be found

My lover lost me,

Yesterday,

And I was freed.

Why does it still hurt so much?

Is it my heart twinging?

Or

Did I break a bone?

Broken beyond repair

Do you believe in love? - they asked

I said “those who feel, believe – I don’t”.

Things you can't return

Take away my name,

And the fame,

Take away all my relationships,

My friends and family,

Take away all that you can.

Just return me my heart.

More

He demanded more.

“you are not enough,

too ordinary,

you are like other millions” - he said.

“what I thought of you was extraordinary” – said I.

The hypocrite me

I endorse human-hood,

Yet I don't respect me.

I endorse love.

Yet I stay with him – who doesn't love me.

I endorse honesty,

Yet I lie to myself every day.

I endorse living to the fullest,

Yet I die every day.

Respect

You gave me flowers -

Those lovely evenings,

The pleasant drives,

You delighted me with gifts.

You made me feel loved,

You gave me everything -

But

Respect.

Deeper wounds

It's strange what a mind captures -

In details.

I remember that silky slip,

When I ran to hold him

Forever.

Then again, I remember

the silky slip -

When I was running away

from him.

Today, my heels hurt me,

Like a dabbing needle,

Yet, it makes me forget my wounds.

Burning I

Was it just me -

Or

The world was burning again.

It was all burning,

Yet there was no smoke.

Burning II

Let’s burn -

Together.

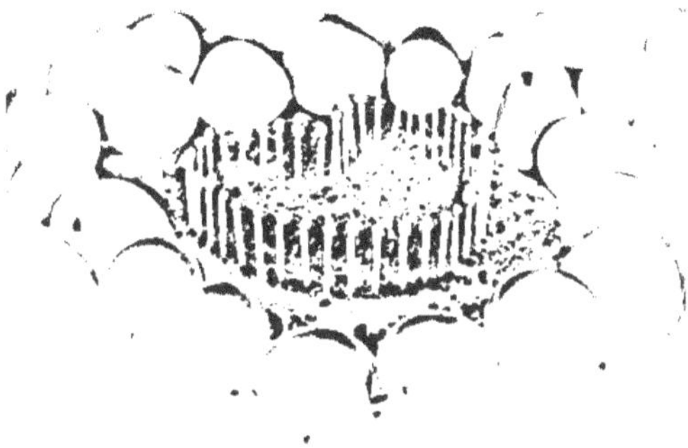

Depression

The walls of my big bathroom - don't flood with my tears.

The pillow of my bed – can soak it all.

The expensive cosmetics – can erase all the worry lines.

Those thick eyeliners – hide the pain.

The bright clothes – hide the rage.

And lo!

I thought I was all alone in this – everyday.

The night

The night is full of pain,

He is saying hurtful things.

I keep it a secret – my darkness,

I keep it quite – my screams,

I keep it dry – my fears,

I know – it will pass,

All I want is to get through the night.

No

Do you know how it feels to feel like me?

Do I know how it feel to feel like you?

NO.

Although we are not together

Although we are not together and will never be,

Don’t pursue -

I might hold on to you, breaking off the present chains.

It was never about love,

It was the friendliness I treasure the most.

When I look at you from far,

While you hold on to someone else’s hand,

The smile on your dimpled cheeks,

Makes me content.

Although we are not together and will never be,

Don’t meet up with me - when alone.

I don’t trust myself around you.

Ours is like an old leaf stuck between the pages,

Crippled, adamant yet, scented.

Book II

Bliss and Verse.

Happiness & Healing.

The dawn helped the deadly night to a beautiful day. Similarly, the human mind can help you drift from your slump to a happy place. As one enters a place of acceptance, actions transform to inspiration. We suddenly feel the shift in energy; a hot day turns into a warm breeze.

The next section of poems is a model for subverting mind questions. Even the temporary answers might free oneself to new heights. Let's celebrate this wild freedom with verbal experiments. I recommend we all try to spend a day by ourselves, every once in a while!

Happy mind I

I am happy in my dream -

at least.

Searching

My bones ache – weary.

My mind still wanders around, with no sign of rest,

Who am I?

My body

Or

Mind?

Healing

Love making, holding hands and kissing are no longer acts of love, but to heal.

Free mind

Once I tasted freedom

Oh!

I don’t know how to live without!

The society I live in, truly confuses me

What do they mean when they ask, "when are you planning to settle down?" I say, "I don't want to settle down. Why will I! There is love in my blood, desires in the air I breath, passion in my eyes and wings of liberation. I do not see the point in "settling down".

Don't people "settle down" only when they die?

(life wonderings)

Stranger

Ironically,

It is easier to be yourself with strangers.

The familiars - just know a lot of you,

And have judged a lot of it.

Being rich

I don't understand the concept of "growing rich".

I feel rich when I have so little,

And,

I felt poorest when I had everything.

Happy mind II

The anchor of my boat is tied – here

Yet, I set my mind miles away -

Yes! I dream....

Wise words

Those who want to stay together, they stay together. Because they love each other and they don't know any other way to live. There are no differences, no barriers, no broken past, no age apart, no "right situation".

I say, if you desperately want to be with someone, just be. Keep the rest to be figured out by "life".

Pretty perfect picture

Once upon a time,

There lived a girl.

"I am happy" - she said,

As she looked in the mirror.

So full of life – energy,

She knew how she wanted to feel,

She looked around – she saw love everywhere,

She was committed to live her dream.

(not every poem is metaphorical)

Mom & Dad

I take intense pride in acknowledging my makers for who I am today. It is not about loving me or giving me the right education or nurturing me, oh that's common! It about setting an example of love, forgiveness and purity of heart. I never had the need to learn from books or school teachers, I just had to look around in my home. Forever grateful.

This is a personal section in this book, yet general to all those wonderful daughters out there. There is no doubt about the love we hold for them, yet there is never a time to rightly express it. We always know, that they know. But I doubt if it were true.

I miss you, Dad

The only difficult part of growing up,

Was leaving my father.

For new job,

For new life,

For new relationships,

For new adventures.

It was that day when I was hurt -

I thought - time will heal.

I will be ok,

But it is this day,

It still hurts.

Every day

I was a new life,

The day you decided to love me whatsoever – every day.

I knew love,

The day you revealed the purity of compassion – every day.

I knew peace,

The day you forgave my flaws – everyday.

My calm father

I have stared at the blue sea -

Too long.

Only to realize,

Its wild beneath.

It’s the same when I look at him.

Lessons for life

I came home upset as my teacher scolded me. I was four. My father came to me. He simply said – “it is important for you to be happy”. I asked, perplexed with big tears in my small eyes, - “why”? He explained that he believes that if I am not happy, everyone surrounding me will be sad. What good could ever happen in such a place? He further justified recalling that mom was unhappy yesterday and so the window glass broke. That moment, my body felt as if someone shook me. Thereafter, I became my hero, I took the responsibility to stay happy and protect my home (not many glasses broke since).

After 20 years, as I recall the incident. My father taught me two things that day. One, happiness comes from a happy determined mind. Two, only you can make yourself happy.

Mom

How did you do it right?

All at a time!

You cooked – amazing,

You taught – fair,

You smiled – as you cared,

You cared – as you gave,

You worked – determined,

You loved – unconditionally,

Yet you never failed.

How did you do it all right?

All at a time!

Mom – Dad

She smells of fresh cream -

He smells of mud.

Two elements, if combined -

Cannot be separated.

Mixed delicately by power,

Sense and Sensibility.

She is the strength behind me,

He is the strength behind her.

Teachings

My father taught me everything -

But,

How to not be myself.

And that is demanded most out of me.

Period.

Treat Right! I

I am the daughter of a King,

The first love of his Queen,

The pride of their only son.

Tell me,

How do I let anyone mistreat me?

Treat right! II

I don’t remember faces; I remember their words.

I don’t remember eyes; I remember their screams.

Treat right III

The greatest gift you can give

Your clan

Your friends

Your fellow souls

Is to treat them right!

No matter what and how much it takes,

Treat right and fight back when mistreated.

Period.

City & God

There is a profuse connect with the divine, experienced through our surrounding or the region we belong to. Hence, the name of this section. If God is everywhere, then cities or the places we dwell in are his little spellbinding toy setup. Of course, the surprises and mysteries he binds us with, are as fascinating.

The city I live in

You are everywhere I see,

You are the shine,

On all faces.

I am lost in you

And you are lost in my ballet.

Busy Indian streets

Do you see what I see?

All eyes eagerly disturbed – hopeful.

A whole chaos – weak directions,

Smell of sweat and weed – all making the air divine to breathe.

His puppet

I am not dismayed

The mystery of "future" -

Fascinates me.

The older I become,

The better I get tamed.

To run His play -

It's true,

"we plan

and He laughs".

Human wisdom is a lie in the eyes of the Maker

Who does justice to mankind?

State or God.

Who is the killer?

The one who kills the body,

Or,

The one who kills the soul.

Who is guilty in the eyes of State?

Who is guilty in the eyes of God?

Readers don't die

When I die,

Don't pray to God for my peace.

Visit me -

My soul,

In between the pages of my books.

You will know,

Yourself -

I am at peace.

Prayers I

Unhappiness is directly

Proportional to age.

When unhappy, you age years within weeks.

When happy, you age days within years.

Keep us young, Almighty!

The heart decides

On the river bank,

Sat a little boy – weeping.

I saw and thought -

What should I do?

My reflex wanted to ask - the reason for the pain.

My mind wanted - to know the problem!

My body wanted to ask - if he was hurt!

Probably, a priest would have shared some wise words.

Yet I decided -

To sit there and weep with him.

Prayers II

I had a deal with Him. I prayed every day, so, shall He remain immortal. So, shall He rule the world and its people. In return just give me back what is mine. A place in the heart of the man I love. Who knew, only I would keep my part of the promise.

Mystery

The questions are many,

But answers none -

It's His mystery that keeps us going.

Why don't we look for stars when the sun is up?

Why does the moth go to the light – only to burn to death?

Why are we the most afraid of the only person we love?

Why does sunflowers turn to each other when the sun is down?

How to feel patient when you feel longing?

The questions are many,

But answers none -

It's His mystery that keeps us going.

Confusing self

I live two lives at a times. One is what I am and one is what I think I am. Both are not the same, of course. Sometimes I am everything but not what my eyes see in the mirror. Sometimes I don't feel myself in my own skin and yet other times I hear someone else while I speak. While I enjoy both my lives, it gets knotty when I try to make them meet.

Only He can make me see who I am. Confusing self is a joy.

Balanced

In this forest of calms,

The fierce wind thunders loud.

The thin stream of blood,

Parting the woods into two.

The deer runs for her life,

The hare runs – thinking the deer is coming for his life.

Yet when the moon lit the night,

They all found peace, where they were once scared.

To be Continued.